100 AMAZING FACTS ABOUT NORWAY

A Collection of Amazing Facts about NORWAY

DEAR VALUED CUSTOMER

Thank you for purchasing this book, can't wait to see your insights and reactions unfold as you dive into its pages.

We sincerely hope you've been enjoying our enchanting book. Your opinion matters greatly to us, and we kindly ask if you could take a moment to share your thoughts by leaving a review on Amazon.

A quick review would be fantastic. It only takes 5 seconds and supports small businesses like ours.

★★★★★

Grab your BONUS e-Book by Scanning the QR code below

Chapter 1: Geography and Nature

Norway is renowned for its stunning fjords, which are long, narrow inlets with steep sides or cliffs, carved by glacial activity. The country boasts over 1,000 fjords, the most famous being the UNESCO-listed Geirangerfjord and Nærøyfjord.

The highest peak in Norway is Galdhøpiggen, standing at 2,469 meters (8,100 feet) above sea level. It is part of the Jotunheimen mountain range and offers breathtaking views of the surrounding landscape.

Norway is home to Europe's largest glacier, Jostedalsbreen, covering an area of approximately 487 square kilometers (188 square miles). It's a captivating sight and a testament to the country's glacial history.

3

The country's coastline is remarkably indented, stretching over 83,000 kilometers (over 51,000 miles) when including fjords and islands. This extensive coastline is longer than that of the United States when measured in proportion to Norway's landmass.

4

With its abundance of wilderness, Norway is a haven for wildlife enthusiasts. The country is home to diverse species such as reindeer, moose, lynx, wolves, brown bears, and the Arctic fox, which thrives in the northern regions.

5

Chapter 2: Culture and Traditions

Norway's national day, known as "Constitution Day" or "Syttende Mai," is celebrated on May 17th. It commemorates the signing of the Norwegian Constitution in 1814 and is marked with parades, traditional costumes (bunads), and festivities nationwide.

The Sami people, indigenous to the Arctic regions of Norway, Sweden, Finland, and Russia, have a rich cultural heritage. They are known for their distinctive clothing, handicrafts like duodji (traditional crafts), and joik, a form of traditional song.

Norwegians have a deep appreciation for nature, known as "friluftsliv," which translates to "open-air living." This philosophy emphasizes spending time outdoors, engaging in activities like hiking, skiing, camping, and fishing, regardless of the weather.

Norway is famous for its folklore, including tales of trolls, mythical creatures believed to dwell in forests and mountains. These stories have been passed down through generations and are a significant part of Norwegian cultural heritage.

The Norwegian language has two official written forms: Bokmål and Nynorsk. Bokmål, meaning "book language," is based on Danish-influenced Norwegian, while Nynorsk, meaning "new Norwegian," is rooted in rural dialects and was developed to preserve Norway's linguistic diversity.

Chapter 3: History and Heritage

The Viking Age, spanning from the late 8th to the mid-11th centuries, was a pivotal period in Norwegian history. Norwegian Vikings, known for their seafaring prowess, exploration, and trading, left a lasting legacy across Europe and beyond.

The famous Viking ships, such as the Oseberg and Gokstad ships, provide invaluable insights into Norse craftsmanship and maritime technology. These well-preserved vessels were buried as part of elaborate funerary rituals and later unearthed in archaeological excavations.

Norway was unified as a kingdom in the 9th century under King Harald Fairhair, who is often regarded as the country's first monarch. His victory at the Battle of Hafrsfjord is considered a defining moment in Norwegian history.

During the Middle Ages, Norway was part of the Kalmar Union, a political union that also included Denmark and Sweden. This period saw the consolidation of Norwegian territory and the emergence of Bergen as a prominent Hanseatic trading city.

The Norwegian Constitution, drafted at Eidsvoll in 1814, laid the foundation for Norway's independence from Denmark. Despite initially entering into a union with Sweden, Norway peacefully dissolved the union in 1905, establishing itself as a sovereign nation.

Chapter 4: Modern Norway

Norway is known for its high standard of living and social welfare system. It consistently ranks among the top countries in global quality of life indices, with universal healthcare, comprehensive social security, and free education up to university level.

16

The discovery of oil and gas reserves in the North Sea in the 1960s transformed Norway's economy. The Norwegian government established the Government Pension Fund Global, also known as the "Oil Fund," to manage revenues from petroleum activities for future generations.

17

Norway is a global leader in renewable energy, particularly hydropower. Approximately 99% of its electricity is generated from renewable sources, making it one of the most environmentally friendly countries in the world.

18

The Nobel Peace Prize, awarded annually in Oslo, Norway, is one of the most prestigious international awards. It was established by the inventor of dynamite, Alfred Nobel, and honors individuals and organizations that have made significant contributions to peace.

Norway is renowned for its modern architecture and design. Iconic landmarks such as the Oslo Opera House, designed by Snøhetta, and the Holmenkollen Ski Jump showcase the country's innovative approach to blending functionality with aesthetics.

20

Chapter 5: Cuisine and Culinary Traditions

Norwegian cuisine is heavily influenced by its maritime heritage and access to fresh seafood. Traditional dishes include "rakfisk" (fermented trout), "lutefisk" (dried cod treated with lye), and "klippfisk" (dried and salted cod).

"Smørbrød," open-faced sandwiches topped with a variety of ingredients such as shrimp, smoked salmon, or pickled herring, are a staple of Norwegian cuisine. They are often enjoyed for breakfast or as a light lunch.

Despite its reputation for cold climates, Norway has a thriving dairy industry. Norwegian cheeses like "Gudbrandsdalsost" and "Brunost" (brown cheese) are popular both domestically and internationally for their rich, caramel-like flavor.

23

"Koldtbord," a Norwegian-style buffet, is a festive culinary tradition featuring an array of cold dishes such as cured meats, smoked fish, pickled vegetables, and assorted cheeses. It's commonly served during holidays and celebrations.

24

Norwegians have a sweet tooth, with pastries like "kanelboller" (cinnamon buns), "skillingsboller" (sweet yeast rolls), and "krumkake" (thin, crispy waffle-like cookies) being beloved treats enjoyed with coffee or tea.

Chapter 6: Notable Norwegians

Edvard Grieg, Norway's most celebrated composer, is renowned for his classical music compositions inspired by Norwegian folk traditions and landscapes. His iconic piece, "Peer Gynt Suite," remains a cornerstone of Norwegian cultural heritage.

Henrik Ibsen, often referred to as the "father of modern drama," was a Norwegian playwright and poet whose works, including "A Doll's House" and "Hedda Gabler," continue to be performed worldwide. His plays challenged societal norms and explored themes of individualism and morality.

Roald Amundsen, a Norwegian explorer, was the first person to reach the South Pole in 1911, leading the Antarctic expedition that achieved this historic feat. His meticulous planning, innovative techniques, and determination made him a pioneer of polar exploration.

28

Thor Heyerdahl gained international fame for his daring expeditions, most notably the Kon-Tiki expedition in 1947. Sailing across the Pacific Ocean on a balsa wood raft, Heyerdahl sought to prove that pre-Columbian South Americans could have reached Polynesia by sea.

Sonja Henie, a Norwegian figure skater and actress, dominated the sport in the 1920s and 1930s, winning three Olympic gold medals and ten World Championships. She later transitioned to Hollywood, starring in successful ice-skating musical films.

Chapter 7: Norse Mythology and Legends

Norse mythology, the ancient belief system of the Scandinavian people, is rich with gods, goddesses, and mythical creatures. Odin, Thor, and Freyja are among the most prominent figures in Norse pantheon, revered for their roles in shaping the cosmos.

The Viking belief in an afterlife was intricately tied to notions of valor and honor. Warriors who died in battle were believed to be taken to Valhalla, Odin's majestic hall in Asgard, where they would feast and prepare for Ragnarök, the end of the world.

The story of Ragnarök, the apocalyptic event in Norse mythology, foretells the ultimate battle between gods and giants, resulting in the destruction and subsequent rebirth of the world. This cataclysmic event symbolizes the cyclical nature of existence.

Yggdrasil, the World Tree, is a central symbol in Norse cosmology, representing the interconnectedness of the nine realms, including Asgard (home of the gods), Midgard (the human realm), and Helheim (the realm of the dead).

34

Loki, the trickster god, plays a pivotal role in Norse mythology as both a cunning ally and a disruptive force. His unpredictable nature and penchant for mischief often lead to conflicts with other gods, culminating in his role as a catalyst for Ragnarök.

35

Chapter 8: Norwegian Inventions and Innovations

The paper clip, a ubiquitous office supply worldwide, was invented by Norwegian Johan Vaaler in the late 19th century. His design, patented in 1899, laid the groundwork for the modern paper clip used today.

36

The cheese slicer, or "ostehøvel," was invented by Norwegian carpenter Thor Bjørklund in 1925. This simple yet ingenious device revolutionized the way cheese is sliced, making it easier and more efficient for households and restaurants alike.

37

The aerosol spray can, a staple in household products and personal care items, was co-invented by Norwegian engineer Erik Rotheim in 1927. His innovative design paved the way for the widespread use of aerosol dispensers across various industries.

38

The gas turbine, a key component in power generation and aviation, was developed by Norwegian engineer Ægidius Elling in the early 20th century. His pioneering work laid the foundation for the modern gas turbine technology used in turbines and jet engines today.

39

The modern salmon farming industry traces its roots to Norway, where innovative aquaculture techniques were developed in the 1960s. Norwegian salmon farming practices have since become a global standard, meeting the growing demand for high-quality seafood.

Chapter 9: Norwegian Exploration and Adventure

The Norse explorers, led by Leif Erikson, are believed to have reached North America around the 10th century, establishing settlements in present-day Newfoundland, Canada. This pre-Columbian contact predates Christopher Columbus's voyages by nearly 500 years.

41

Fridtjof Nansen, a Norwegian explorer, scientist, and diplomat, became the first person to traverse the Greenland ice cap in 1888. His daring expedition laid the groundwork for modern polar exploration and earned him international acclaim.

42

The legendary explorer, Roald Amundsen, achieved another milestone in polar exploration when he became the first person to reach the North Pole in 1926. His successful expedition aboard the airship Norge solidified his status as one of the greatest explorers of his time.

43

Thor Heyerdahl's Kon-Tiki expedition captured the world's imagination in 1947 when he and his crew sailed across the Pacific Ocean on a balsa wood raft. The voyage sought to prove Heyerdahl's theory that ancient South Americans could have reached Polynesia by sea.

44

In 1994, Norwegian adventurer Børge Ousland became the first person to complete a solo unsupported crossing of Antarctica. His grueling 1,674-kilometer (1,040-mile) journey across the frozen continent showcased human endurance and determination.

45

Chapter 10: Norwegian Arts and Literature

"Peer Gynt," a play written by Henrik Ibsen, is one of Norway's most beloved literary works. Inspired by Norwegian folk tales, the play tells the story of the titular character's journey through life, love, and self-discovery.

Edvard Munch, a Norwegian painter and printmaker, is best known for his iconic work "The Scream." This expressionist masterpiece, depicting a figure in distress against a swirling sky, has become a symbol of existential angst and modern art.

The Norwegian black metal music scene gained international notoriety in the 1990s for its extreme sound, controversial lyrics, and provocative imagery. Bands like Mayhem, Burzum, and Emperor pioneered the genre, leaving a lasting impact on heavy metal music worldwide.

Jo Nesbø, a Norwegian author, is acclaimed for his gripping crime novels featuring detective Harry Hole. Nesbø's intricately plotted thrillers, set against the backdrop of Oslo's gritty underworld, have earned him a global following and critical acclaim.

The Norwegian playwright and filmmaker, Joachim Trier, has garnered praise for his thought-provoking films exploring themes of identity, desire, and existentialism. Works such as "Reprise," "Oslo, August 31st," and "Thelma" have cemented his reputation as a leading voice in Scandinavian cinema.

Chapter 11: Norwegian Wildlife and Conservation

The Norwegian Arctic archipelago of Svalbard is home to one of the world's largest polar bear populations. These majestic creatures roam the sea ice in search of seals, their primary prey, making Svalbard a hotspot for wildlife enthusiasts and researchers.

Norway's coastal waters are teeming with marine life, including whales, dolphins, seals, and a variety of seabirds. The nutrient-rich waters support diverse ecosystems, making whale watching and wildlife cruises popular activities along the Norwegian coast.

52

The Norwegian government has implemented strict conservation measures to protect its natural environment and biodiversity. National parks, nature reserves, and marine protected areas safeguard critical habitats and species, ensuring their long-term survival.

53

The reintroduction of the European beaver, once extinct in Norway, has been a conservation success story. Through careful management and habitat restoration efforts, beavers have returned to Norwegian rivers and wetlands, contributing to ecosystem health and biodiversity.

54

Norway is committed to sustainable fisheries management, balancing the needs of fishermen with the conservation of fish stocks and marine ecosystems. Strict quotas, gear regulations, and seasonal closures help ensure the long-term viability of Norway's fisheries.

55

Chapter 12: Norwegian Royalty and Monarchy

The Norwegian monarchy traces its roots back to the Viking Age, with the first recorded Norwegian king, Harald Fairhair, reigning in the 9th century. Since then, Norway has had a long line of monarchs, including the current reigning King Harald V.

King Harald V ascended to the throne in 1991, following the death of his father, King Olav V. He and his wife, Queen Sonja, are widely respected for their dedication to public service and their efforts to modernize the monarchy while preserving its traditions.

57

Crown Prince Haakon, the heir apparent to the Norwegian throne, is known for his advocacy on social and environmental issues. He and his wife, Crown Princess Mette-Marit, are actively involved in charitable organizations and initiatives promoting sustainability and youth empowerment.

58

The Norwegian royal family resides primarily at the Royal Palace in Oslo, although they also have several other residences, including Skaugum Estate and Bygdøy Royal Farm. These historic properties serve as official residences and venues for royal events and ceremonies.

Norway's monarchy enjoys widespread support and respect among the Norwegian people, with the royal family playing a unifying role in national life. Celebrations such as National Day and royal weddings are eagerly anticipated and attended by citizens from all walks of life.

Chapter 13: Norwegian Sports and Outdoor Activities

Cross-country skiing is a national pastime in Norway, with generations of Norwegians learning to ski at a young age. The country's extensive network of groomed trails, known as "løyper," provides opportunities for skiers of all abilities to explore the winter landscape.

Biathlon, a combination of cross-country skiing and rifle shooting, has a strong following in Norway. The country has produced numerous Olympic champions and world-class athletes in this demanding sport, which requires both physical endurance and precision marksmanship.

62

Ski jumping is another winter sport in which Norway excels, with a rich history dating back to the 19th century. Iconic venues like the Holmenkollen Ski Jump in Oslo host international competitions and attract spectators from around the world.

Sailing and boating are popular recreational activities in Norway, thanks to the country's extensive coastline, fjords, and lakes. From leisurely cruises along the fjords to exhilarating regattas and offshore racing, there are options for sailors of all skill levels.

64

Hiking and trekking opportunities abound in Norway's vast wilderness, with countless trails crisscrossing mountains, forests, and coastal landscapes. The country's national parks and nature reserves offer hikers the chance to experience pristine nature and breathtaking scenery.

Chapter 14: Norwegian Education and Innovation

Norway places a strong emphasis on education, with a publicly funded education system that provides free primary and secondary education for all children. Higher education is also heavily subsidized, with universities and colleges offering a wide range of degree programs.

The Norwegian education system is known for its student-centered approach and emphasis on critical thinking, creativity, and collaboration. Inquiry-based learning methods encourage students to explore concepts actively and develop problem-solving skills.

67

Norway consistently ranks among the top countries in the world for innovation and research. The government invests heavily in science and technology, supporting initiatives to drive innovation in fields such as renewable energy, biotechnology, and information technology.

Norwegian universities and research institutions are at the forefront of groundbreaking discoveries and advancements in various fields. Collaborative research projects and partnerships with industry leaders contribute to Norway's reputation as a hub for innovation and knowledge exchange.

The Norwegian Centre for Research Data (NSD) is a leading institution for data management and research infrastructure services. It provides valuable resources and support to researchers, enabling them to conduct high-quality research and advance knowledge in their respective fields.

Chapter 15: Norwegian Holidays and Festivals

Christmas is a cherished holiday in Norway, marked by festive traditions and customs. Norwegians celebrate with family gatherings, traditional meals like "ribbe" (roast pork belly), and the lighting of advent candles to count down to the holiday season.

71

Easter is another significant holiday in Norway, known for its unique traditions such as "påskekrim" (Easter crime novels) and outdoor activities like skiing and cabin trips. Families often decorate eggs and participate in Easter egg hunts, known as "påskeeggjakt."

Midsummer's Eve, or "Sankthansaften," is celebrated in Norway with bonfires, outdoor gatherings, and festivities. It marks the summer solstice and is believed to have pagan origins, with bonfires lit to ward off evil spirits and celebrate the abundance of the season.

73

Constitution Day, or "Syttende Mai," is Norway's national day and a time of patriotic celebration. Parades featuring marching bands, schoolchildren in traditional costumes, and flag-waving crowds fill the streets as Norwegians commemorate the signing of their constitution in 1814.

74

The Sami National Day, held on February 6th, celebrates Sami culture, language, and heritage. Festivities include traditional music and dance performances, reindeer races, and exhibitions showcasing Sami handicrafts and cuisine.

Chapter 16: Norwegian Language and Literature

Old Norse, the language of the Vikings, evolved into the modern Norwegian language spoken today. While Norwegian is the official language, there are also distinct regional dialects reflecting the country's diverse cultural heritage.

Norwegian literature has a rich tradition dating back to the medieval sagas and ballads. The works of authors such as Henrik Ibsen, Knut Hamsun, and Sigrid Undset have achieved international acclaim and continue to inspire readers worldwide.

The Norwegian playwright, Henrik Ibsen, is often regarded as one of the greatest dramatists in world literature. His plays, which include "A Doll's House," "Ghosts," and "Hedda Gabler," explore complex psychological themes and societal issues with timeless relevance.

Knut Hamsun, a Nobel laureate in literature, is best known for his novel "Hunger," a groundbreaking work of psychological realism. His writing style, characterized by vivid imagery and introspective narration, influenced generations of writers and filmmakers.

Sigrid Undset, another Nobel laureate, is celebrated for her historical novels set in medieval Norway. Her masterpiece, "Kristin Lavransdatter," chronicles the life of a Norwegian woman from childhood to old age, offering a vivid portrait of medieval society and values.

Chapter 17: Norwegian Fashion and Design

Norwegian fashion combines elements of traditional craftsmanship with contemporary design aesthetics, resulting in a unique and distinctive style. From knitwear and outdoor apparel to minimalist accessories, Norwegian designers draw inspiration from nature and heritage.

The Norwegian sweater, or "norsk genser," is an iconic garment known for its intricate patterns and warm, woolen construction. Traditional designs such as the "Selbuvotter" (Selbu mittens) and "Setesdal" pattern have become synonymous with Norwegian knitting traditions.

The bunad, Norway's national costume, varies in style and design across different regions of the country. Each bunad is meticulously crafted and adorned with embroidery, silver jewelry, and other embellishments that reflect local traditions and cultural heritage.

83

Norwegian footwear brands like Viking and Alfa are renowned for their durable and functional outdoor footwear. Whether hiking in the mountains or braving the winter cold, Norwegians rely on quality footwear to navigate the rugged terrain and inclement weather.

Scandinavian design principles, characterized by simplicity, functionality, and minimalism, have had a profound influence on global design trends. Norwegian designers like Andreas Engesvik, Kristine Five Melvær, and Lars Beller Fjetland continue to uphold these principles in their work.

Chapter 18: Norwegian Technology and Innovation

Norway is a world leader in maritime technology and offshore engineering, with companies like Kongsberg Maritime and DNV GL driving innovation in shipbuilding, navigation systems, and offshore energy production.

The development of electric vehicles (EVs) and renewable energy solutions is a priority for Norway's green transition. The country boasts one of the highest rates of EV adoption in the world, thanks to incentives such as tax breaks, toll exemptions, and extensive charging infrastructure.

Norwegian companies like Equinor (formerly Statoil) are at the forefront of offshore wind energy development, harnessing the power of the North Sea to generate clean electricity. Offshore wind farms such as Hywind Scotland showcase Norway's expertise in renewable energy technology.

Norway's commitment to sustainability extends to the construction industry, where innovative green building practices are gaining traction. Passive house design, energy-efficient materials, and sustainable construction methods contribute to the country's goal of reducing carbon emissions.

89

The Norwegian Space Agency (NOSA) collaborates with international partners on space exploration projects and satellite missions. Norway's expertise in satellite technology and remote sensing applications supports efforts to monitor climate change, natural disasters, and environmental phenomena.

Chapter 19: Norwegian Music and Performing Arts

Traditional Norwegian music, known as "folkemusikk," encompasses a wide range of styles and instruments, including the Hardanger fiddle, accordion, and langeleik (a type of zither). Folk music festivals and gatherings celebrate Norway's rich musical heritage.

91

Grieg's compositions drew inspiration from Norwegian folk melodies and landscapes, capturing the essence of the country's natural beauty in his music. Pieces like "Morning Mood" from the Peer Gynt Suite evoke the tranquility of Norway's fjords and mountains.

The Oslo Opera House, inaugurated in 2008, is a striking architectural landmark and cultural hub for the performing arts. Its state-of-the-art facilities host opera, ballet, concerts, and theatrical productions, attracting world-class performers and audiences alike.

Norwegian theater companies like Det Norske Teatret and Den Nationale Scene showcase a diverse range of productions, from classic dramas to contemporary works. Theater festivals and fringe events promote emerging talent and push the boundaries of artistic expression.

Chapter 20: Norwegian Mythology and Folklore

The Nøkken, a malevolent water spirit, is said to inhabit lakes, rivers, and ponds in Norwegian folklore. Often depicted as a shapeshifter or a handsome young man, the Nøkken lures unsuspecting victims to their watery demise with its mesmerizing music.

95

The Huldra, a seductive forest spirit, is a recurring figure in Norwegian folklore. With her long, flowing hair and cow's tail, she entices travelers deep into the forest, only to reveal her true, troll-like form and disappear into the wilderness.

96

The Draugen, an undead creature resembling a drowned sailor, is believed to haunt the coastal waters of Norway. Sailors who encounter the Draugen at sea are said to be cursed with misfortune or death, making it a feared and respected figure in maritime lore.

The Nisse, a mischievous household spirit, plays a central role in Norwegian Christmas traditions. Believed to live in barns and stables, the Nisse rewards kindness with good fortune but punishes neglect or disrespect with pranks and mischief.

98

The Troll, a staple of Norwegian folklore, is a fearsome creature known for its size, strength, and propensity for mischief. Trolls are said to dwell in remote mountains and forests, emerging from their hiding places at night to wreak havoc on unsuspecting travelers.

99

Chapter 21: Norwegian Fashion and Textile Industry

The Norwegian wool industry has a long history dating back centuries, with sheep farming and wool production playing a significant role in rural economies. Norwegian wool is prized for its warmth, durability, and natural insulating properties, making it ideal for cold weather apparel.

100

Conclusion

Exploring Norway's 100 fascinating facts unveils a nation brimming with history, beauty, and innovation—from Viking sagas to eco-friendly endeavors. As our journey concludes, let Norway's allure spark a deep appreciation for its culture and global impact.

Printed in Great Britain
by Amazon